Written by Patrick Geistdoerfer
Illustrated by Joëlle Boucher

Specialist adviser:
Dr. Patrick Geistdoerfer is a senior
staffer at the National Center
for Scientific Research (France)

ISBN 0-944589-02-2
First U.S. Publication 1988 by
Young Discovery Library
217 Main St. • Ossining, NY 10562

Undersea Giants

YOUNG DISCOVERY LIBRARY

Many stories, like the ones about Jonah or Pinocchio, tell of men who were swallowed by whales.

The story of Jonah tells us that after having been thrown into the sea, he was swallowed by a big fish.

Then Jonah was thrown up on the shore. Others have invented similar tales.

How do you identify
whales and dolphins?
They are not fish
even if they resemble
them. Fish breathe
in water. Whales
and dolphins
come up to the
surface to breathe
air. But they
always live in the
sea and never come
onto the land. Whales are so big
that men were once afraid of them.
However, whales do not
eat men!

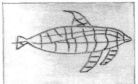

A Stone Age engraving
of a dolphin

Dolphin painted in Crete
4,000 years ago.

The whale is pictured
as a monster in this
old engraving.

Dolphins are much smaller. They
often come near the shore, or swim
around boats, without fearing man.

Whales and dolphins
form the group of
aquatic creatures
known as **cetaceans.**
They are **mammals.**

In ancient times, dolphins were sacred.
This one is carrying a god on its back.

Here are the whales, the biggest of the cetaceans. They do not have teeth but baleen, which permits them to filter food.

Bowhead whale

Finback whale

Blue rorqual
or blue whale

Baleen consist of long strips of bone. There can be 3,000 of them, and some measure ten feet in height.

Humpback whale

Right whale

The other cetaceans all have teeth.
Some are very big, like the sperm whale, and others are smaller, like the dolphin.

Dolphin

Orca, or killer whale

Narwhal or unicorn whale: its one tooth forms a defense!

The beluga is dark gray at birth, then it becomes spotted. By four or five years old, it is all white!

Sperm whale

Beluga

Cetaceans live in all the oceans of the world. They spend the summer in cold areas where they find more food. In the winter, they are in the warm seas where their young are born.

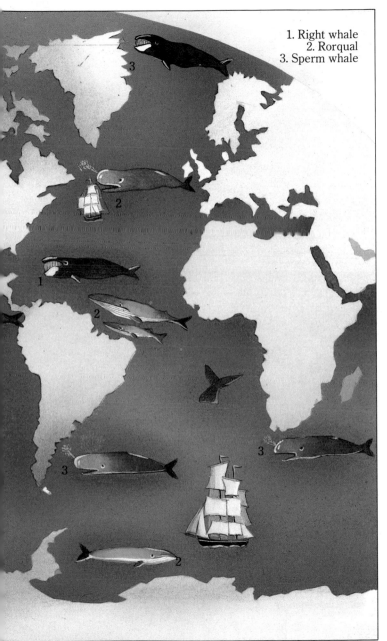

1. Right whale
2. Rorqual
3. Sperm whale

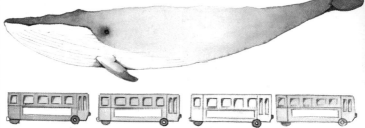

The blue whale is the biggest and heaviest animal in the world.

It can measure 100 feet long, as much as four buses put end to end! It weighs as much as thirty elephants, more than a hundred and thirty tons...

Its tongue alone is as heavy as an elephant! The sperm whale and the right whale measure about sixty five feet. The dolphin is much smaller: only six to nine feet long!

The heaviest land animal is the elephant. It weighs about four tons and reaches about thirteen feet in height.

Skeletons of a whale and of a rorqual

In place of our arms, whales have flippers in which are found the same bones as ours. They move forward thanks to the powerful beatings of their tails.
The whale and the dolphin have smooth, thin skin. Underneath they have an enormous layer of fat.

How do they breathe?
They come to the surface and expel the air contained in their lungs. The air leaves by one or two holes at the top of the skull. It is mixed with water vapor and forms a spray: it is the **blow** of the whale.

A whale blows.

Dorsal fin of an orca.

Tail of a finback

Dolphins and whales live in herds, or pods, sometimes as large as several hundred animals. One of them serves as a guide.

Why do they jump? To give the alarm, show their strength, or attract females. The little ones seem to jump to play!

The jumps of the big cetaceans are spectacular and very noisy. This whale does a half flip in the air before landing on his back.

Different jumps of the humpback whale.

The cetaceans are able to dive deeply and for a long time.

Dolphins make a series of very rapid jumps. They can swim at more than thirty miles an hour.

The sperm whale holds the record for dives: it dives more than 3,000 feet deep and stays for up to an hour and a half underwater!

Birth of a little dolphin

Its mother carries it on her back.

The biggest newborn in the world.

After a ten month wait, the blue rorqual gives birth to a baby whale over 21 feet long, weighing eight tons! She immediately pushes it to the surface so it can breathe.

The female dolphin nurses her little one for sixteen months.

Other females help her to carry it.

How are the little cetaceans nourished?

Under water, milk from the mother's teats (nipples) is squirted into the baby's mouth. The milk is very rich in fat: in one week the baby doubles its weight! At this rate, it gets a good layer of fat quickly to protect it from the cold when it goes to the polar waters.

It will live twenty or thirty years.

The blue rorqual is able to eat up to two
thousand pounds of small animals in one meal.

With its baleen, the whale is not
able to chew or swallow. It
gobbles down thousands of tiny
shrimp and little fish. The water
comes out through a hedge of baleen
which retains the little animals
like an enormous sieve.

Sperm whale food:
squid and fish.

The sperm whale feeds on fish and especially squid, the animals with long tentacles.
The biggest ones will fight when the sperm whale grabs them with its teeth. But the battle is unequal.
The squid ends up eaten!

The orca is a fierce hunter.

It is also called the killer whale! But really it is a very big dolphin. Orcas live in groups of about ten animals. They are easily recognized by the big fin on their backs; it sticks up out of the water. Orcas hunt fish and squid and also sharks, seals, dolphins and birds. They do not attack divers. They are **voracious** eaters: the remains of eleven seals and thirteen porpoises were found in one orca's stomach.

A seagull

A seal

Orcas even hunt whales!

Orcas attack in a herd. They bite the whale with sharply pointed teeth. The whale has no chance to escape them!

A dolphin

The dolphin is very intelligent.
It seems to play when it races with
boats. It learns tricks easily, like
standing up on its tail and jumping
in the water. Perhaps you will see
dolphins and orcas leaping in an aquarium
by the seashore. They are fun to watch,
but this captive life condemns them to
an early death.

A real language.
Dolphins and whales make numerous
sounds which permit them to talk to
each other: they whistle, grunt...
They hear very well. Sailors say
that whales sing! Dolphins and
whales avoid obstacles while emitting
very high-pitched sounds, too high-
pitched for you to hear them! These
sounds bounce back from the obstacle
to the cetacean, indicating what is
in front, even if it is not seen.

Why did men hunt whales so much?

Because their enormous bodies were a great source of riches!

Their melted fat made oil, used in lamps in olden days. Today it is made into margarine, soap...
The baleen was used to make umbrella ribs, still called umbrella whales!
In the skull of the sperm whale, one finds **spermaceti** which is used in medicines, candles and cosmetics.
The meat from the whale is eaten.

The cutting up of a stranded sperm whale

After making use of many whales grounded on beaches, men hunted them on all the seas of the world.

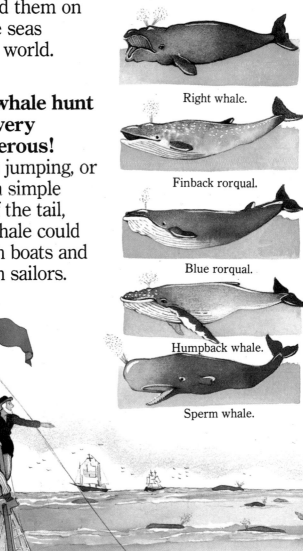

Right whale.

The whale hunt was very dangerous!
While jumping, or with a simple flip of the tail, the whale could smash boats and drown sailors.

Finback rorqual.

Blue rorqual.

Humpback whale.

Sperm whale.

From high on the mast, the lookout cries: There she blows! Then the crew prepares. Light boats called whaleboats are put into the water. They hurry towards the whale. The harpooner is in the bow. His harpoon is attached to the boat by a long solid line.

As soon as the whaleboat is close
enough, the man throws his harpoon so
it sticks in the flesh of the whale.
Wounded, the whale fights, sometimes
dives. It flees, dragging the
whaleboat behind it at high speed.
The race can last for hours. But the
whale eventually gets tired and ends
up dying under the stabbing of the
sailors' lances.

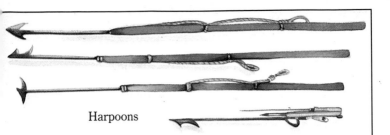

Harpoons

Sometimes, as in the Azores, islands
in the North Atlantic, the hunters
wait on land. The lookouts
on the cliffs signal
when they see the whales.
Immediately, the boats,
ready and waiting on
the beaches, are put
into the water. After
the catch, the whalers
tie the whale's body alongside
the boats and return to shore.
The fat, called **blubber,** is cut into
strips and melted in
big pots.
The oil is then
put into barrels.

Engraved
whale's
tooth

A 19th century
whaling ship.

A modern hunt is done by fleets of powerful boats over 100 feet long. They have a harpoon cannon on the prow. This harpoon contains a shell that explodes when it hits the whale, wounding it seriously. The boats drag their catch to the factory vessel. The whale is hoisted into the ship through an opening at the back, then it is lifted up to the deck, and carved up.

The hunting boat tows its prey.

The factory ship hoists the whale and fastens it to the deck.

Because of hunting, the number of whales has greatly decreased. **We must hunt whales less.** There are now laws about hunting, and only a few countries, like Japan, still hunt whales.

Here are some other mammals that live in the sea!

Sea lions have external ears while seals do not have any.

They spend part of the time on the beaches or the ice floes. They can stay under water about twenty minutes. Their skin is covered with fur. They eat fish, crabs, shellfish or seabirds. The biggest of these animals is the sea elephant: it can weigh more than three tons and measure twenty feet long.

The walrus has enormous upper tusks which form its defense.

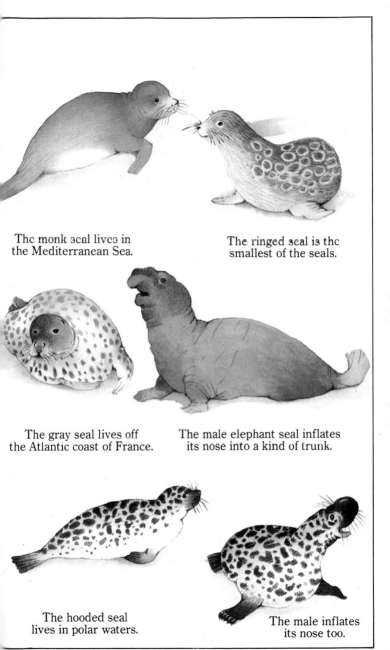

The monk seal lives in the Mediterranean Sea.

The ringed seal is the smallest of the seals.

The gray seal lives off the Atlantic coast of France.

The male elephant seal inflates its nose into a kind of trunk.

The hooded seal lives in polar waters.

The male inflates its nose too.

The Whale

Our gallant ship her anchor weighed,
   And to the sea she bore away,
    Brave boys,
   And to the sea she bore away.

Old Shouter was our captain's name,
   Our ship the *Lion* bold,
And we were bound to the North Country
   To face the frost and cold.

And when we came to that cold country
    Where the ice and snow do lie,
Where there's ice and snow, and the
    great whales blow,
And the daylight does not die,

Our mate went up to the topmast head
    With a spyglass in his hand:
"A whale, a whale, a whale," he cries,
    And she spouts at every span."

We struck that fish and away she flew
    With a flourish of her tail;
But oh! and alas! we lost one man
    An we did not catch that whale.

Now when the news to our captain came
    He called up all his crew,
And for the losing of that man
    He down his colors drew.

Now the losing of that sailor boy
    It grieved our captain sore,
But the losing of that mighty whale
    It grieved him even more.

                            Old Sea Shanty

Index